Learning at Home

Together We Can: Pandemic

By Shannon Stocker

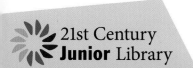

21st Century
Junior Library

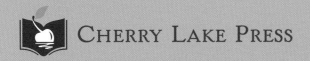

Published in the United States of America by Cherry Lake Publishing Group
Ann Arbor, Michigan
www.cherrylakepublishing.com

Reading Adviser: Marla Conn, MS, Ed., Literacy specialist, Read-Ability, Inc.

Photo Credits: © Alexander_Safonov/Shutterstock.com, cover, 1; © Monkey Business Images/Shutterstock.com, 4, 12; © Leonard Zhukovsky/Shutterstock.com, 6; © Studio Romantic/Shutterstock.com, 8; © Africa Studio/Shutterstock.com, 10; © R R/Shutterstock.com, 14; © Brocreative/Shutterstock.com, 16; © Gorodenkoff/Shutterstock.com, 18; © wavebreakmedia/Shutterstock.com, 20

Library of Congress Cataloging-in-Publication Data

Names: Stocker, Shannon, author.
Title: Learning at home / Shannon Stocker.
Description: Ann Arbor, Michigan : Cherry Lake Publishing, 2021. | Series: Together we can. Pandemic | Includes index. | Audience: Grades 2-3 | Summary: "The COVID-19 pandemic introduced many changes into children's lives. Learning at Home looks at the disruption of their school routines and gives actionable suggestions to help young readers adapt as we navigate the current outbreak. This includes science content, based on current CDC recommendations, as well as social emotional content to help with personal wellness and development of empathy. All books in the 21st Century Junior Library encourage readers to think critically and creatively, and use their problem-solving skills. Book includes table of contents, sidebars, glossary, index, and author biography"—Provided by publisher.
Identifiers: LCCN 2020039973 (print) | LCCN 2020039974 (ebook) | ISBN 9781534180109 (hardcover) | ISBN 9781534181816 (paperback) | ISBN 9781534181113 (pdf) | ISBN 9781534182820 (ebook)
Subjects: LCSH: Web-based instruction—Juvenile literature. | Homebound instruction—Juvenile literature. | COVID-19 (Disease)—Juvenile literature.
Classification: LCC LB1044.87 .S8466 2021 (print) | LCC LB1044.87 (ebook) | DDC 371.33/44678—dc23
LC record available at https://lccn.loc.gov/2020039973
LC ebook record available at https://lccn.loc.gov/2020039974

Cherry Lake Publishing Group would like to acknowledge the work of the Partnership for 21st Century Learning, a Network of Battelle for Kids. Please visit http://www.battelleforkids.org/networks/p21 for more information.

Printed in the United States of America
Corporate Graphics

CONTENTS

What are some benefits of staying at home?

Why We're Staying Home

When a **pandemic** happens, like the **coronavirus**, it can feel like the world is shutting down. Schools close, and many parents have to work from home.

While extra time at home might seem fun at first, a **quarantine** can create all kinds of challenges. If you're used to going to school every day, one of the biggest challenges is adjusting to learning from home.

Most schools in the United States closed when the virus first appeared.

Even people who feel perfectly healthy have to **social distance** during a pandemic. Some viruses, like the coronavirus, can be sneaky. They can make some people feel bad, while other people remain completely **asymptomatic**. Yet even though asymptomatic people don't feel sick, they can still **transmit** the virus to others. That's why social distancing only works if we all do it. And it's why school may be unsafe for many families.

Ask Questions!

Are there things you'd like to know about the pandemic? Ask away! Understanding situations can help you feel more comfortable and less afraid.

Many teachers will answer questions on Zoom or FaceTime!

Staying home during a pandemic is the best way you can help your friends and family. But what does that mean for school? It means students and teachers must find new ways to have class. Sometimes, teachers may record a unit for you to watch online. Sometimes, you may be able to join a live class online with your classmates! Other times, your teacher may send homework through email and expect you to email the finished work back.

Put your schedule where you can see it every day.

A Need for Routine

When you're at school, you have a routine every day. When you're learning from home, you should also have a routine! Do you like to talk with friends? Then make time for a video call with a classmate or teacher! Do you wiggle and wriggle a lot? Then give yourself room to move! Spend more time learning about the things you love! You can't skip the subjects you don't like, but you'll probably enjoy activities more when you help plan them.

Wake up and have breakfast at the same time every day.

Are there **tangible** things you loved in your classroom at school? If so, create a work space with those things at home. Did you sit on a yoga ball? Did you have crayons on your desk? When your learning environment feels familiar, you will be more likely to feel comfortable. And don't forget to try to make your space free of **distractions**!

Think!

What things made you feel comfortable at school? What was your favorite poster in the room? Your favorite book? Did you have a class pet?

For a change of pace, do math problems outside with sidewalk chalk!

Help plan your day the night before! When creating your schedule, remember to include time for meals and snacks, exercise, baths, and play. Don't plan for more than you can handle. Try to schedule schoolwork in 20-minute chunks. Then take at least 10 minutes between work sessions to give your mind and body a break.

Exercising makes for a great break! It's good for your body and your mind.

Make It Fun!

Did you know that learning at home doesn't stop with schoolwork? It's true! Challenge yourself to make time for creativity every day. Learn how to do a cartwheel or how to cook. Maybe you always wanted to learn how to draw! There are lots of YouTube videos or library books that can help you learn all sorts of new skills.

School might look different this year, but you can still see friends!

Do you like to read? Start a book club! You and a friend could read the same book **simultaneously**, even though you're far apart. When you're finished, you can plan a virtual meeting to talk about your favorite parts.

Make a Guess!

How do you think your teachers are adjusting to new school routines? What about your parents? Ask and find out!

Your grown-ups at home want to make this school
year as good as possible!

Learning at home can be hard for everyone. Most parents aren't teachers, so they're learning too. But with a little extra planning, and with your help, you can make your day a whole lot more fun together!

GLOSSARY

asymptomatic (ay-simp-tuh-MAH-tik) having no symptoms of a disease

coronavirus (kuh-ROH-nuh-vye-ruhs) a family of viruses that cause a variety of illnesses in people and other mammals

distractions (dih-STRAKT-shuhnz) things that take your attention away from what you are doing

pandemic (pan-DEM-ik) an outbreak of a disease that affects a large part of the population

quarantine (KWOR-uhn-teen) the state of being isolated from others

simultaneously (sye-muhl-TAY-nee-uhs-lee) at the same time

social distance (SOH-shuhl DIS-tuhns) to stay at least 6 feet (2 meters) away from others

tangible (TANJ-ih-buhl) things that can be touched

transmit (trans-MIT) to pass from one person or place to another

FIND OUT MORE

WEBSITES

Brain Pop—Create More "Aha!" Moments Together
https://www.brainpop.com

Common Sense Media—Dance Games
https://www.commonsensemedia.org/lists/dance-games

IXL—Personalized Learning
https://www.ixl.com

Khan Academy
https://www.khanacademy.org

YouTube—Art for Kids Hub
https://www.youtube.com/user/ArtforKidsHub

YouTube—Cosmic Kids Yoga
https://www.youtube.com/user/CosmicKidsYoga

INDEX

ABOUT THE AUTHOR

Shannon Stocker writes picture books, books for young readers, and *Chicken Soup* stories. Her favorite parts of learning at home have been finding and identifying plants, flowers, snakes, birds, and other critters around her house with her children. Shannon lives in Louisville, Kentucky, with Greg, Cassidy, Tye, and far too many pets.